S0-AKW-200

Exploring Science

The Exploring Science series is designed to familiarize young students with science topics taught in grades 4–9. The topics in each book are divided into knowledge and understanding sections, followed by exploration by means of simple projects or experiments. The topics are also sequenced from easiest to more complex, and should be worked through until the correct level of attainment for the age and ability of the student is reached. Carefully planned Test Yourself questions at the end of each topic allow the student to gain a sense of achievement on mastering the subject.

EXPLORING
THE HUMAN BODY

Ed Catherall

RAINTREE
STECK-VAUGHN
L I B R A R Y
The Steck-Vaughn Company

Austin, Texas

Exploring Science

Library of Congress Cataloging-in-Publication Data

Catherall, Ed.
   The human body / written by Ed Catherall.
     p.   cm. — (Exploring science)
   Includes index.
   Summary: Describes different parts of the body and their
functions. Includes related activities and review questions.
   ISBN 0-8114-2599-1
   1. Body, Human—Juvenile literature.   2. Health—Juvenile
literature.   [1. Body, Human.]   I. Title.   II. Series: Catherall,
Ed.   Exploring science.
QP37.C34   1992   91-19983
612—dc20   CIP
                                    AC

Cover illustrations:
Left *An artist's impression of the human skeleton in motion.*
Above right *A doctor listens through a stethoscope to a baby's heartbeat.*
Below right *A diagram showing the human heart.*
Frontispiece *If you fall and cut yourself, white blood cells rush to the wound and fight
bacteria entering the bloodstream through the broken skin.*

Editor: Elizabeth Spiers
Editor, American Edition: Susan Wilson
Series Designer: Ross George

Typeset by Multifacit Graphics, Keyport, NJ
Printed in Italy by G. Canale & C.S.p.A., Turin
Bound in the United States by Lake Book, Melrose Park, IL

1 2 3 4 5 6 7 8 9 0 Ca 97 96 95 94 93 92

Contents

YOUR BODY

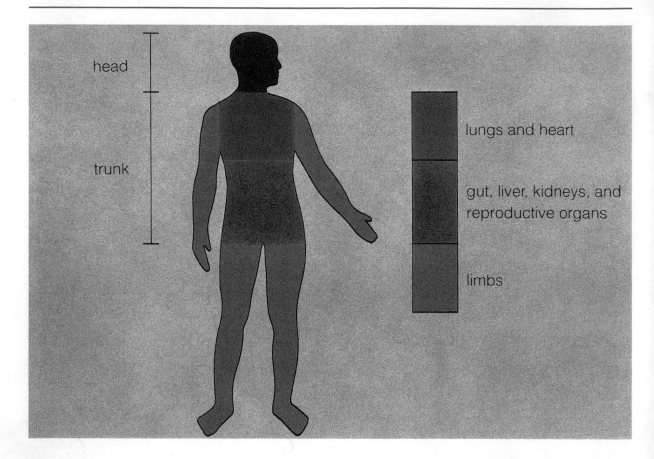

head

trunk

lungs and heart

gut, liver, kidneys, and reproductive organs

limbs

Your body is the most important thing in your life. It is very complicated, and scientists spend a lot of time and money finding out how it works. There are many tasks that it performs: it can eat, breathe, grow, repair itself, move, and get rid of wastes and harmful substances. The body protects itself from illness and damage. The human body also reacts to its surroundings. It can think and learn. It can also reproduce itself. For the body to work well, it must be well cared for.

Your body consists of a head, trunk, and limbs. Your head contains some extremely important parts. One of these parts, your brain, controls your entire body. The air that you breathe and the food that you eat are taken in through your head. You communicate mostly with your head: by speaking, by the expressions on your face, and by your hearing. You also find out about your environment with your head—by smell, sight, and taste.

Your trunk is divided into two sections. The upper half contains the lungs and heart; the lower part contains the gut, liver, kidneys, and reproductive organs. Your four limbs are for movement and receiving information by touch. They also help you to balance.

ACTIVITY
YOUR BODY SHAPE

YOU NEED

- **a large sheet of paper**
- **crayons**
- **a tape measure**

1 Lie on your back on the sheet of paper.

2 Ask a friend to trace around your body.

3 Use the tape measure to find out the length and width of your head and trunk from the outline. Record these measurements.

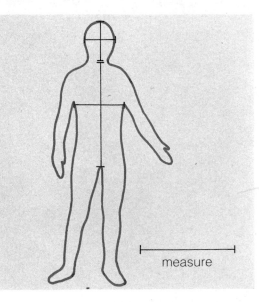

measure

4 Measure and record the length and width of your arms and legs.

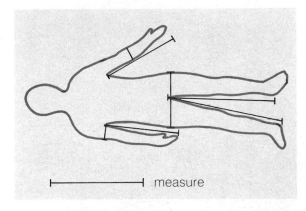

measure

5 Compare these measurements with those of several friends. Make a set of bar graphs to show how the measurements vary. (Do a different bar graph for each type of measurement.)

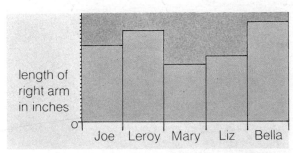

length of right arm in inches

Joe   Leroy   Mary   Liz   Bella

6 Study your bar graphs. Is there a pattern? For example, does the person with the largest head have the longest arms?

TEST YOURSELF

1. Which parts of your head help you to find out about your surroundings?

2. Name six tasks that your body performs.

3. How many pairs of limbs do you have? Name something that your upper limbs can do that your lower limbs cannot.

CELLS

Your body is made up of tiny building blocks called cells. An adult has more than one trillion of these tiny cells. There are many different kinds of cells, each with its own special job to do; but, in general, they all perform the same basic tasks. Cells take in food and produce energy needed by your body to work, to make materials called proteins for repair and growth, and to reproduce (make copies of themselves). The different types of cells are arranged to make tissues and organs. For example, some cells form the pipes that make up your blood vessels; others form your muscles.

Most of your cells do not last for your entire life. They die and are replaced. In general, the only cells that cannot reproduce and replace themselves are your nerve cells. Nerve cells die off gradually, so that by the time you die you have fewer than when you were born. Some cells, such as the ones on the surface of your skin,

live for only a few days. Your red blood cells (see page 26) last for about four months, while bone cells may live for twenty-five years.

Each of your cells, except for your sex cells, is able to make an exact copy of itself by dividing in two. Children have far fewer cells than adults. As you grow, more and more cells are added to those you already have. When you are fully grown, your cells reproduce themselves at a slower rate, mainly replacing those that die.

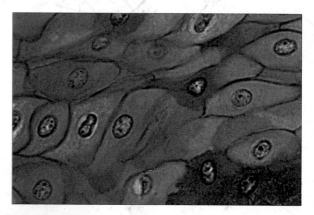

Above Cells from the tissue that covers the outer layers of the body. This type of tissue also lines the tubes inside your body, such as the gut.

Left A cell found in part of the brain.

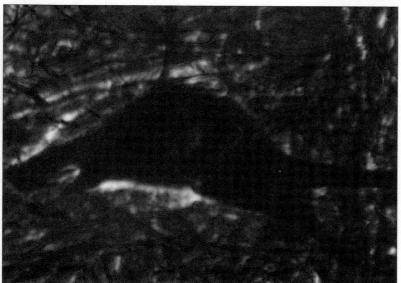

ACTIVITY
LOOKING AT CELLS

YOU NEED

- **a clean toothpick**
- **a dropper (pipette)**
- **2 microscope slides**
- **glass cover slips**
- **a microscope**
- **an onion**
- **a sharp knife**

WARNING: You must get an adult to help when using the knife. You must also be very careful with the glass slides and cover slips.

1 Rinse out your mouth with water.
2 Gently scrape the toothpick against the inside of your cheek.
3 Use the dropper to place a drop of water on a slide. Swirl the toothpick in the water. Then break the toothpick and discard.
4 Cover the scrapings with a cover slip.

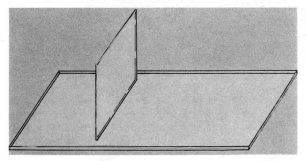

5 Look at the cheek scrapings under the microscope. Through the strongest lens, you should be able to see some small, roundish shapes. These are cells from your cheek. Draw what you see.

6 Ask an adult to cut the onion and peel off a very thin layer. Place a little of this on the other slide.
7 Use the pipette to put a drop of water on the onion.

8 Cover the onion and water with a cover slip.
9 Look at the onion through the microscope. You should see what looks like bricks in a wall. These are the cells that make up the onion. Draw them.

TEST YOURSELF

1. What are most cells able to do?
2. How long do red blood cells live?
3. Which cells cannot replace themselves?

YOUR SKELETON

Inside your body, you have a skeleton made of bones joined together. A skeleton serves three major functions. First, the skeleton serves as a strong support for the large human body. Second, the skeleton protects the softer organs and tissues of the body from injury. Third, the bones of the skeleton serve as anchors for the muscles, and thus allow movement (see page 14). The bones of the skeleton also perform two other functions. They provide a place where blood cells can be made, and they store a substance your body needs, called calcium (see page 18).

Your skull is made up of several bones all joined together forming a box that protects your brain and eyes. If you have a skeleton at school, look at the skull and you will see these pieces of bone, fitted together like a jigsaw puzzle. In the trunk of your body, you can feel your rib cage, pelvis (hips), shoulders, and spine (backbone). The rib cage protects your heart and lungs, while your pelvis helps to support the weight of your body. It also protects some of the soft organs in the lower part of your trunk. Your spine is the main support for your body. It is made up of a column of bones called vertebrae. The string of small bones makes your spine flexible or able to be bent. Imagine trying to tie your shoelaces if your spine were made of just one long bone! Your spine also protects your spinal cord, which links the brain with the rest of your nervous system (see page 34).

A diagram of the human skeleton.

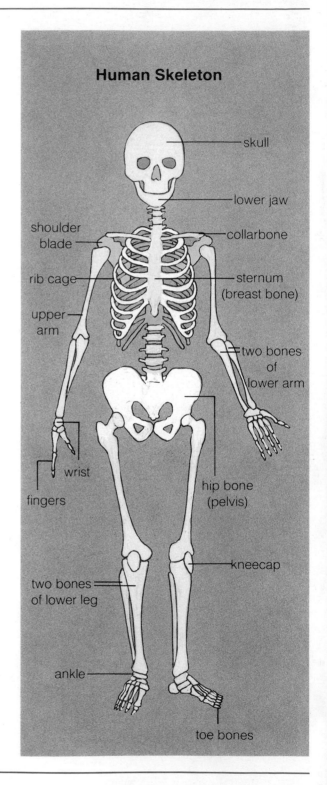

Human Skeleton

skull

lower jaw

shoulder blade

collarbone

rib cage

sternum (breast bone)

upper arm

two bones of lower arm

wrist

fingers

hip bone (pelvis)

kneecap

two bones of lower leg

ankle

toe bones

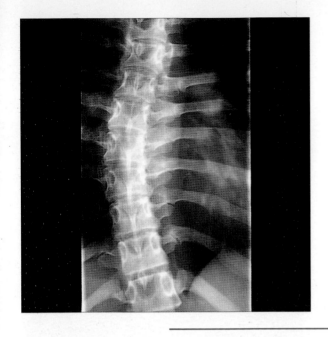

An X ray of part of the spine, showing the vertebrae and part of the spinal cord.

Your arms are called upper limbs and are attached to the spine by the shoulder blades. At the ends of your arms, your hands are attached by the wrists. There are a large number of bones in your wrists and hands; like the spine, this helps to make them flexible. They can perform complicated movements, such as writing. Your legs, or lower limbs, are also connected to the spine, by your pelvis. Your feet are attached to your legs by the ankles. The ankles and feet have many small bones that make them flexible.

ACTIVITY

YOU NEED

- **a diagram of the human skeleton**
- **body outline used on page 7**
- **colored pencils**

1 Work with a friend.
2 Use the diagram of the human skeleton to draw the positions of your bones inside your outline.
3 Label the bones. Choose different colors for bones that protect, bones that support, and limbs.

Remember that some bones protect and support. Use another color to label these.
4 Make a key (guide) to show what the different colors means.

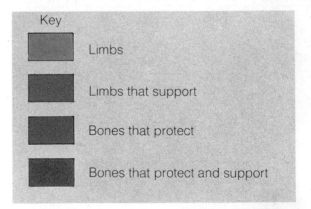

Key

Limbs

Limbs that support

Bones that protect

Bones that protect and support

TEST YOURSELF

1. Give three functions of your skeleton.
2. Which bones protect your heart and lungs?
3. Which are vertebrae?
4. Why is the wrist such a flexible joint?

BONES AND JOINTS

You have three main types of bones: long, short, and flat. They are all covered by a hard shell and are soft and spongy inside. Long bones are found in your arms, legs, fingers, and toes. Inside, they have a substance called marrow, which makes red and some white blood cells (see page 26). Your backbone, ankles, and wrists have short bones. These contain a network of long, thin fibers, like girders in a building. Flat bones make up your skull, ribs, and shoulder blades and have a thin spongy layer in the middle.

Bones are connected to each other by joints. Joints allow the bones to move while they protect the bones from rubbing together. There are

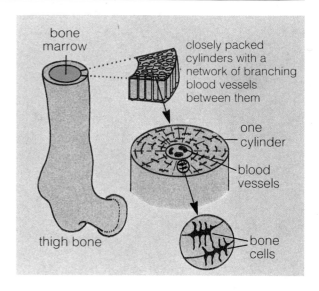

A cross section through the thigh bone.

several different kinds of joints. Most are either hinge joints or ball-and-socket joints. Hinge joints are found in places such as the elbow and fingers. These joints allow movement mostly in one direction. Ball-and-socket joints are in the hips and shoulders. They allow much more movement. There are also other kinds of joints, such as those found between the bones in your spine. These bones have disks of spongy tissue between them that work like shock absorbers in a car. Another type of joint that allows almost no movement is found between the two bones in your forearm.

Joints that allow a lot of movement are protected from wear and tear. The ends of the bones are covered in a smooth layer called cartilage. The

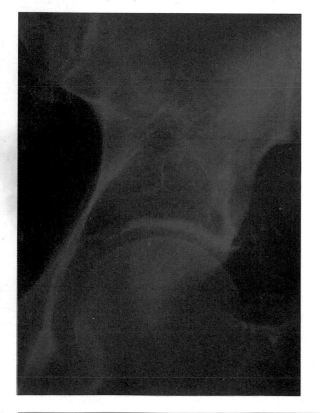

An X ray taken through the pelvis. It shows the ball-and-socket joint, where the top of the thigh bone joins the pelvis.

whole joint is covered in an envelope, or capsule that contains thick fibers called ligaments. They help to strengthen the capsule and keep the bones in position. The capsule secretes (gives out) a slippery fluid that lubricates the joint, like oil on a bicycle chain.

ACTIVITY

INVESTIGATING YOUR JOINTS

WARNING: be careful when making the movements in this activity. Joints are easily damaged.

1 Hold one of your arms straight, away from your body. Turn the palm of your hand up.
2 Bend and straighten your elbow. How far does it move? Can your forearm move from side to side?

3 Sit on a chair. Stretch your leg out straight in front of you. How far can you bend your knee? Does your knee let you move your lower leg from side to side?

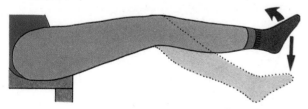

4 Stand up. How far can you swing your leg backward and forward? Can you swing from side to side?
5 Test your shoulder joint by swinging your arm around. What sorts of movements can you make?

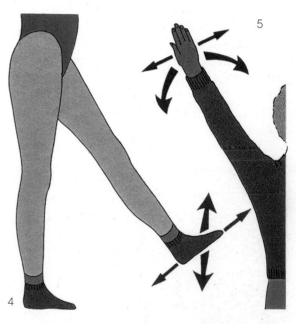

6 What sorts of movements can you make with your fingers?
7 Make a chart showing the joints you have tested, what type of joints they are, and how you can move them.

TEST YOURSELF

1. What are the three main types of bones?
2. Where would you find joints that allow almost no movement?
3. How are joints protected from damage?

MUSCLES AND MOVEMENT

You need to be able to make a large range of movements in your everyday life. Muscles help you to do this. You have two main types in your body: involuntary and voluntary. Involuntary muscles are sometimes called automatic muscles. This is because you have no control over them. Perhaps you do not even know that they are there. Your heart (see page 29) has involuntary muscles to keep it beating. Imagine what life would be like if you had to remember to keep your heart beating! Other involuntary muscles move your food through your digestive system (see page 22).

Voluntary muscles are those that your body deliberately controls, even though you may not think about it. They are attached to your bones, either directly or by thick, strong bundles of fibers called tendons. You can feel one of them, called the Achilles' tendon, in the back of your ankle. However, voluntary muscles do not just move limbs. Your tongue, eyes, and jaw, for instance, cannot move without these muscles.

A microscope photograph of cells found in a muscle.

Your muscles are made up of thin, flexible fibers, and the fibers in one muscle all work together. Each fiber is connected to a nerve (see page 34). The nerve receives messages from your brain, telling the muscle when to contract (shorten) and by how much. When you do not need to use that muscle again, your brain tells all the nerves to relax (lengthen) the muscle fibers.

Your muscles are arranged in groups. The simplest kind of group is used to move hinge joints (see page 12). These have pairs of muscles that are called antagonistic, meaning that they work against each other. For example, if you feel the front of your upper arm, and move your hand toward your face, you will feel your biceps muscle. It bunches as the muscle contracts, pulling your forearm up. Now straighten your arm and feel the muscle relax and become flat. Do this again, but feel the triceps muscle at the back of your upper arm.

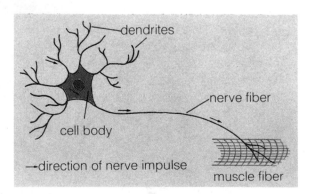

A diagram showing how a nerve cell is attached to a muscle fiber.

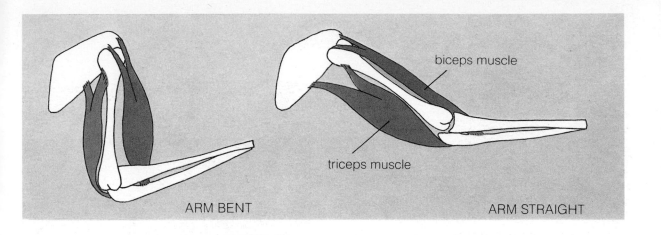

biceps muscle

triceps muscle

ARM BENT   ARM STRAIGHT

ACTIVITY

MAKING A MODEL ARM

YOU NEED

- **cardboard**
- **5 push-through paper fasteners**
- **2 strong rubber bands**
- **2 labels**

1 Cut out two shapes from cardboard, as shown in the diagram.

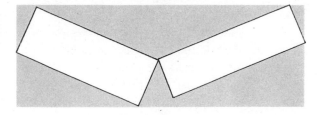

2 Join the shapes with a paper fastener through the "elbow."

3 Connect the shapes with the rubber bands. One band is the biceps and the other is the triceps. Label the rubber bands.

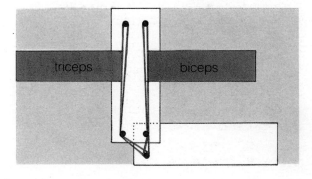

triceps   biceps

4 Bend the model arm. What happens to the biceps and the triceps?

5 Straighten the arm. What happens to the biceps and the triceps?

TEST YOURSELF

1. What are the two kinds of muscle in your body? Give an example of where they are found.

2. Explain why the biceps and triceps muscles of the arm are called antagonistic.

3. Describe how a muscle works.

YOUR DIET

When you hear the word diet, you probably think of someone who is trying to lose weight. But diet really means the food that people eat in their everyday lives. Although people around the world have a great range of diets, most diets contain the same basic foods. The three main foods are carbohydrates, fats, and proteins. Humans also need vitamins, minerals, water, and roughage, or fiber. All these food substances are needed for energy, growth, repair, and general health.

Your body needs a constant supply of energy to perform all its tasks properly. When your muscles move, they are using energy. Your body also uses energy to keep warm, to keep the heart beating, and to keep the brain functioning. Your body is using energy even when you are asleep.

In general, a larger person uses more energy than a smaller person. Because

A chart showing the average amounts of energy required each day by people of different ages and sex.

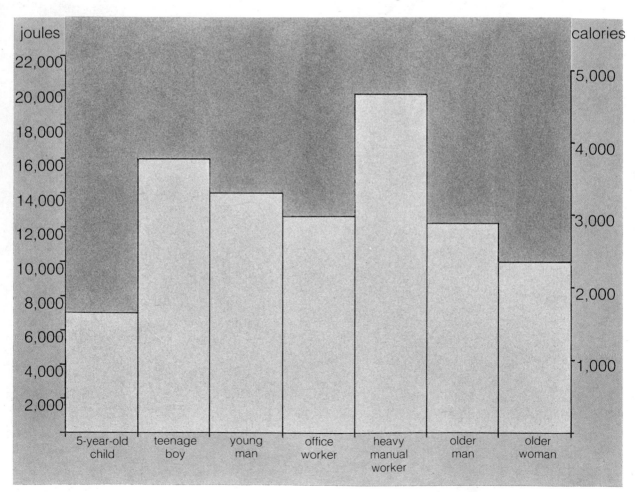

A healthy diet includes fresh fruit and vegetables, lean meat, fish, eggs, milk and yogurt, whole wheat bread, whole wheat cereals, and plenty of water to drink.

men are generally larger than women, most men need to eat more than women do. Pregnant women and women who are breast-feeding need more energy than other women. Young children need less energy, and thus less food, than those who are older. Children over twelve need about the same amount of energy as adults.

Most of a person's energy comes from carbohydrates and fats. The main type of carbohydrate is starch, which is found in rice, potatoes, bread, pasta, and a wide range of cereals. Sugars are also carbohydrates. Fats and oils are found in butter, milk, meat, cheese, fish, and eggs. These are called animal fats. Vegetable fats and oils are found in seeds, such as

sunflower seeds, and some vegetables, such as avocado. Most doctors and scientists think that people should eat only small amounts of fat, particularly animal fat. They believe that high-fat diets cause many problems, including weight gain and heart disease.

Proteins are very important. They are needed to repair the body and help it to grow. Proteins also provide some energy. They are found in fish, eggs, meat, cheese, milk, poultry, and some vegetable products. People who do not eat meat are called vegetarians. They get protein from beans, such as lentils.

We need only tiny amounts of vitamins and minerals. Vitamins are found in foods. There are many types, and without some of them you would become very ill and eventually die. For example, your bones and teeth may not form properly if you do not have the correct vitamins when you are a child. The lack of certain other vitamins causes your eyes, skin, and blood to become unhealthy. Minerals are also vital for life. They can be found in most normal diets. Calcium (for bones and teeth) and iron (for the blood) are both important minerals for healthy bodies.

Water is also essential for life. About three quarters of your body is water. It is found throughout your body. Water in your diet comes from drinking and eating. You could be starved of food for several weeks, but, without water, you would die within a few days.

Most food substances contain some material that cannot be digested (see page 23). This is called dietary fiber, bulk, or roughage. It is very important to have plenty of this in your diet. Doctors and scientists think that it can help prevent cancer of the bowel, and it certainly keeps you from becoming constipated. It is found mainly in fruit, vegetables, and whole-grain products, such as brown rice and whole-wheat bread.

Citrus fruits (such as oranges, lemons, and grapefruit) are an excellent addition to any diet. They contain dietary fiber, lots of water, and natural sugar. Citrus fruits are best known for their high levels of vitamin C.

ACTIVITY

YOU NEED

- **different food record sheets**
- **packaging from foods you have eaten**

1 List all the foods that you have eaten in one day.
2 Use the food record sheets and the package labels to find out whether a food is a carbohydrate, protein, or fat. Which foods contain dietary fiber?
3 Half your food should be carbohydrate; the rest, protein with little fat or oil. Was your diet balanced that day?
4 Plan a menu for next week. List all the foods that you will eat. Have you repeated any meals?
5 Which day do you think contains the most balanced diet?
6 List your favorite foods. Are these foods good for you? Are they part of a balanced diet?
7 Do your friends eat types of food that are different from those you eat? What is different about their food? Are their diets balanced?
8 Find out all you can about the diets of other nations.

| | Monday | | | | |
Time	Food eaten	Carbohydrate	Protein	Fat or oil	Dietary fiber
8:00	Toast				
	Butter				
	Jam				
	Tea				
	Milk				
	Sugar				
11:00	2 Crackers				
	Juice				
12:45	Fish				
	Potatoes				

TEST YOURSELF

1. What are the three main substances found in most diets?
2. What does your body need in order to carry out cell repair, replacement, and growth?
3. Plan a menu for one day that you consider to be a good, balanced diet.

YOUR TEETH

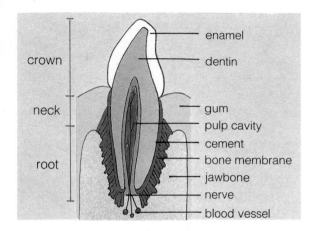

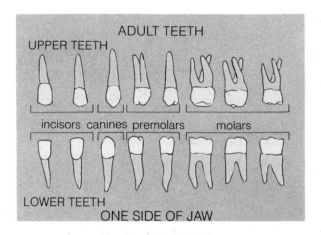

The first part of your digestive system is your teeth. They break food into small pieces that make it easy to swallow and to digest. Two rows of teeth bite, tear, cut, and grind food.

You have two sets of teeth in your life. The first set is called baby teeth, and there are twenty of them. You probably got your first tooth when you were about six months old. And you probably had all twenty baby teeth before you were two years old. When you were about six, your adult teeth started pushing out the baby teeth. Extra ones will grow until you have thirty-two.

Humans have four types of teeth and each type is suited for a special task. Together they allow humans to eat a varied diet. Eight incisors at the front of your mouth cut your food. Next to them are four canines ("dog teeth"). They are used for tearing. At the sides of your mouth, you have eight premolars and twelve molars, which have bumpy surfaces. Your food is ground into small pieces between the molars, and the premolars help with grinding and tearing.

Your teeth are alive. Each tooth is covered by a thin layer of enamel, which is the hardest substance that your body makes. Beneath this is a soft substance called dentin. This contains a pulp cavity, through which the blood vessels and nerves run. Each tooth has roots that fit into a socket in the jawbone. All the teeth are held in place by rubbery gums. The roots of your teeth are held in the sockets by ligaments that take the impact if you bite something hard.

It takes only a few minutes every day to keep your teeth healthy and looking good. Most dental (tooth) disease starts from sticky plaque that covers the teeth. Plaque contains millions of bacteria that make the acid that causes tooth decay. Sugar on your teeth provides food for the bacteria to grow and spread. To prevent tooth decay and gum disease, you must floss and brush you teeth regularly. Most dentists say that you should brush your teeth at least twice a day and visit a dentist every six months for a checkup. If you care for your teeth, they should last you for life.

ACTIVITY

CLEANING YOUR TEETH PROPERLY

YOU NEED

- **a dentist's disclosing tablets**
- **an ordinary mirror**
- **a dentist's mirror**
- **toothpaste**
- **your own toothbrush**
- **a cup**
- **running water**

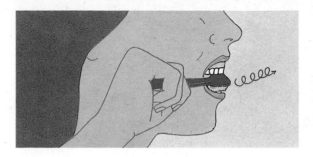

1 Suck a disclosing tablet. This will show all the plaque on your teeth.
2 Look in the mirror. Use your dentist's mirror to examine your teeth. Notice all the areas of plaque that the tablet has stained.

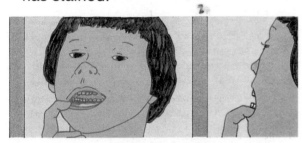

3 Spread some toothpaste on your brush.
4 Hold your brush at an angle to your gums. Brush gently near the top of your teeth, using little circular movements. Watch yourself in the mirror as you do it.

5 Do this for each tooth, in front and behind.
6 Rinse your mouth. Look in the mirror. Were you able to remove most of the stained plaque?
7 Brush over the top surfaces of your teeth with a back-and-forth movement. Use more toothpaste if needed.

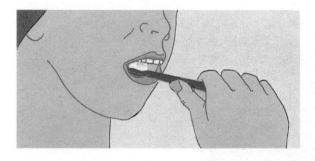

8 Rinse your mouth again. Look at your teeth.
9 If you have not gotten rid of the stain, repeat steps 4 to 8 until all the stain is gone.
10 How long did it take you to do this? Do you usually spend this much time brushing your teeth?

TEST YOURSELF

1. What are the four kinds of adult teeth? How many of each kind are there?
2. What causes teeth to decay?
3. What should you do to keep your teeth healthy?

YOUR DIGESTIVE SYSTEM

The food you eat is broken down into chemicals that your body uses for growth, repair, and energy. Food is broken down by the digestive system, a long tube running through your body. This system has several parts, each with its own task.

Each part of your digestive system contains or produces different chemicals. They help to break down the food and dissolve it in water. These chemicals are called enzymes. Each enzyme works on a particular type of food. Some work only in acid conditions, others need alkali. Cells in the gut walls secrete acid or alkali—whichever is needed. Once the food is broken down, it passes through the gut walls and is carried by the blood to all parts of the body.

As you chew your food, glands in your mouth release saliva. This helps to soften the food, so that it can pass down your gullet, or esophagus, into the stomach. Saliva also contains an enzyme that starts to break down starch. The stomach is the widest part of the digestive tract. Acid in the stomach helps an enzyme break down proteins. The stomach also mashes the food into a soft, runny paste called chyme. The chyme then passes down into the top of the small intestine. Bile, made in the gall bladder and stored in the liver, breaks up oils and fats into tiny droplets. This makes them easier to digest. Another gland, the pancreas, secretes an alkali that helps enzymes digest fats, proteins, and starch. As the food passes farther down the small intestine, other enzymes continue to break it down.

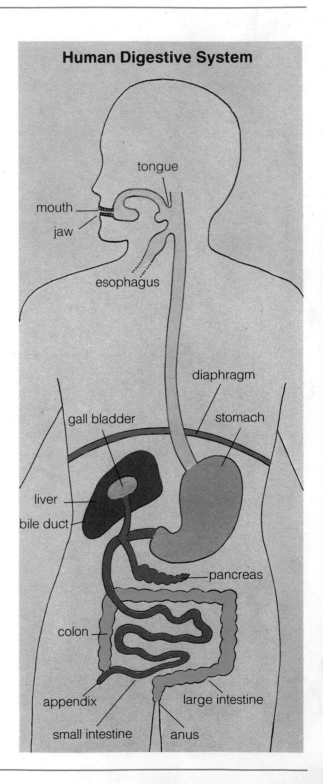

Human Digestive System

tongue

mouth

jaw

esophagus

diaphragm

gall bladder

stomach

liver

bile duct

pancreas

colon

appendix

large intestine

small intestine

anus

Anything that is not digested and absorbed (soaked up) by the gut walls is waste. This is usually dietary fiber (see page 18). Fiber builds up in the large intestine, is passed to the rectum by the squeezing of involuntary muscles (see page 14) and is moved out of the body through the anus.

ACTIVITY

ENZYMES AT WORK

YOU NEED

- **egg white**
- **a covered glass jar**
- **fresh pineapple juice**
- **a white cloth**
- **liverwurst**
- **egg yolk**
- **chocolate**
- **several detergents that contain enzymes**

WARNING: In case you have sensitive skin, wear rubber gloves when using detergents.

1 Put a little egg white in a glass jar. Cover it with pineapple juice. Cover the jar to keep out dust.

2 Shake the jar occasionally. Slowly, enzymes in the juice will dissolve the egg white.

3 Smear small pieces of white cloth with meat paste, egg yolk, and chocolate.

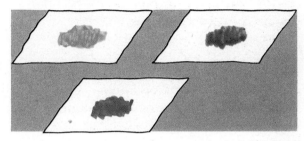

4 Read the instructions on the bottle or box of detergents. Wash each stained cloth in warm water. Do the enzymes dissolve the food stains? Which stain is the hardest to remove? Which detergent works best?

TEST YOURSELF

1. What is the function of the digestive system?
2. What happens to food in your mouth?
3. What does your stomach do?
4. What do enzymes do?

FOOD ABSORPTION

You know that the chemicals from broken-down food have to be dissolved in water so that they can be absorbed through the gut walls. From there they go into your bloodstream, to be taken where they are needed.

Carbohydrates, mainly starch and sugars, are broken down to glucose, which is a chemical that dissolves easily in water and can be absorbed quickly. Proteins are broken down to amino acids, which are also water-soluble. Fats and oils are broken down into tiny droplets that "hang" in water. This is called an emulsion.

The small intestine is where most of the chemicals are absorbed. It is very narrow and can be 20 feet long. Its lining is not smooth but is covered by millions of villi, which are tiny fingerlike projections.

These villi greatly increase the surface area. This means that the surface area through which food chemicals are absorbed is far larger than it would be if it were smooth. The villi contain tiny blood vessels that absorb the nutrients (food chemicals). Cells in the walls of the intestine take in fat and oil droplets.

All the absorbed nutrients travel in the bloodsteam to the liver. The liver is very large and has many tasks. It checks the absorbed nutrients and if there is too much of a particular kind, the liver will store it. The liver breaks down some poisonous or harmful substances, making them less harmful.

Nutrients that are not absorbed by the small intestine move on to the large intestine. Here, water, minerals, and vitamins are absorbed.

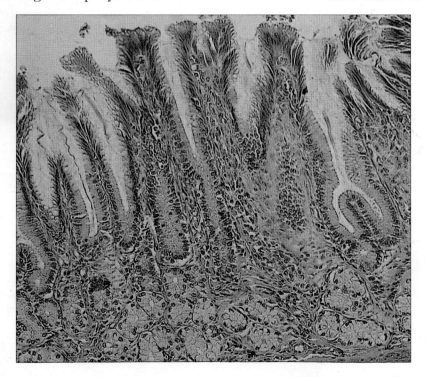

A microscope photograph of the lining of the intestine, showing the fingerlike villi.

ACTIVITY

INCREASING SURFACE AREA

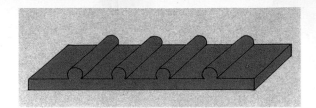

YOU NEED

- **a rolling pin**
- **modeling clay**
- **a kitchen knife**
- **a ruler**
- **a ball of string**
- **a felt-tipped pen**

WARNING: Be careful when using the knife. It does not have to be a sharp one.

1 Use the rolling pin to roll out a fairly large ball of clay.
2 Cut out two strips about 4 inches long and 1 inch wide. Make sure they are both the same length.

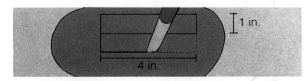

3 Use the rest of the clay to make four sausage shapes as thick as your little finger and about 1 inch long.
4 Stick the "sausages" along one of your strips of clay. This is a model of villi on the walls of the small intestine.

5 Measure and record the length of the flat piece of clay.

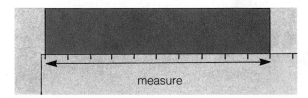

measure

6 Cut a length of string about 20 inches long.
7 Ask a friend to hold one end of the string at one end of the strip with the "sausages." Run the string carefully over the "sausages," touching the clay strip between them. Mark the string with the pen where it touches the other end of the strip.

8 Take the string away and measure it with your ruler. Compare this length to that of the flat strip. What have the model villi done to the surface area of the clay strip?

TEST YOURSELF

1. What are nutrients?
2. How do nutrients get into your bloodstream?
3. What does your liver do?

YOUR BLOOD

You know that nutrients from your food are moved to your cells. Some of this food gives you energy by being "burned" in the cells with oxygen. That oxygen is carried from your lungs to those cells (see page 30). Your body is also protected from disease and wounds are healed. Wastes are taken away from your cells. Your blood does all these jobs.

Blood is made up a watery yellow fluid called plasma, in which float millions of tiny cells. Its red color comes from disk-shaped cells called red blood cells. Billions of red blood cells are carried in your blood. Red blood cells contain a chemical called hemoglobin that picks up oxygen from your lungs and takes it to your cells. If your red blood cells are the wrong shape, or you do not have enough hemoglobin, you have anemia. You look pale and become tired and weak.

Your blood also contains millions of white blood cells. Each cubic millimeter of blood contains 5,000–10,000 of them. They defend your body against bacteria and other harmful materials. There are several different

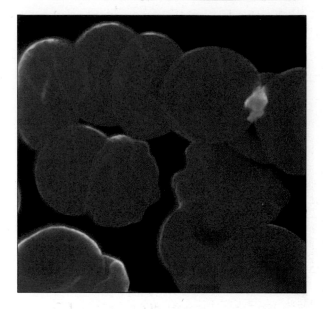

An electron microscope photograph (specially colored) showing red blood cells.

kinds of white blood cells, and each kind specializes in the way it fights disease. Some of the white blood cells do this by attacking and surrounding the foreign particles.

If you have a wound, cells called platelets help to plug the hole. A substance called fibrinogen makes a network of tiny fibers. It does this by turning into fibrin. A scab eventually forms and drops off when the area of skin is mended. White blood cells rush to the wound and fight any bacteria or dangerous substances that enter through broken skin.

If your blood were not continually cleaned, you would become seriously ill and eventually die. Your kidneys perform this task. Every five minutes,

An electron microscope photograph showing a blood clot.

all your blood has passed through your kidneys and has been cleaned. The waste products that your kidney filters out of your blood collect, along with water, in your bladder. This is called urine and is passed out of your body several times a day. An adult usually passes 1 to 1.5 quarts of urine per day, but this amount may be as much as 3 quarts.

ACTIVITY

HOW MUCH BLOOD DO YOU HAVE?

YOU NEED

- **bathroom scale**
- **a calculator**
- **a measuring cup**
- **a dishpan**

INFORMATION: An adult weighing about 150 lbs has about 6 quarts of blood. A small child weighing 25 lbs has about 1 quart of blood. Roughly 25 lbs of body weight is equivalent to 1 quart of blood.

1 Weigh yourself on the bathroom scale. Record your weight to the nearest pound.
2 To figure out how many quarts of blood you have, write down:
    your weight in pounds ÷ 25

Number of quarts of blood =
$$\frac{\text{MY WEIGHT IN POUNDS}}{25}$$

3 Use your calculator to find the answer. Give that answer to the nearest 0.5 (half) quart. Write your answer under the calculation in part 2.

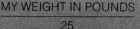

$$\frac{\text{MY WEIGHT IN POUNDS}}{25}$$

$$= ? \text{ QUARTS}$$

4 Figure how many cups of blood you have (4 cups to a quart). Use the measuring cup to pour that much water into the dishpan to see what the volume of your blood looks like.

5 Compare your results with those of others in your class by drawing a bar chart.

TEST YOURSELF

1. What do red blood cells do?
2. How do white blood cells fight foreign particles, such as bacteria?
3. Describe what happens if you cut your knee.

YOUR CIRCULATORY SYSTEM

Blood travels through your body and to your cells in a system of vessels, or tubes. These form a high-speed, one-way transport system around the body. This is called the circulatory system. Blood is forced through this system by the heart.

You have three types of blood vessels—arteries, capillaries, and veins. Vessels carrying blood away from the heart are called arteries. Arteries divide into smaller and smaller branches. The very smallest branches are tiny vessels called capillaries. Capillaries are found throughout the tissues of your body and come in close contact with your cells. Nutrients from your food and oxygen from your lungs pass out of the blood through the thin walls of the capillaries. Waste materials

The entrance to the aorta. This artery takes blood from the heart to all parts of the body except the lungs.

from the cells, such as carbon dioxide, pass back into the blood and are carried away. The blood vessels that return blood to the heart are called veins.

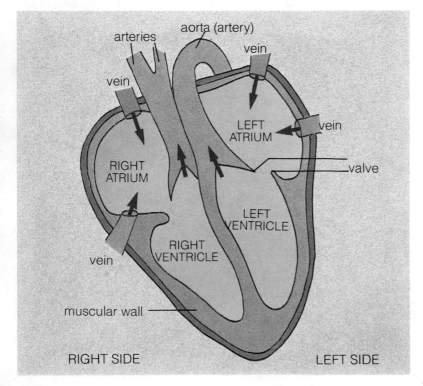

A diagram showing a cross section of the heart.

Blood is very thick and sticky, causing your heart to pump it at high pressure. Your arteries have very thick, elastic walls—they do not burst under this pressure. Compared to the arteries, pressure inside the veins is low. The low pressure could allow blood to flow backward, toward the capillaries. Flaps called valves prevent any backward flow.

Your heart is very muscular and strong—it has to beat about once every second for your whole life. The heart is really two separate pumps, side by side. Each pump has two compartments—an atrium (plural: atria) and a ventricle. The ventricle is the main pump—it has very thick walls. The atrium receives blood from the veins and forces the blood a short distance to the ventricle. The walls of the atrium are thin. Valves between the atrium and ventricle prevent blood from flowing backward. There are also valves at the outlets of the ventricles.

There are two parts to your circulation. Blood from your right ventricle flows along an artery to the lungs, where the blood picks up oxygen. From there, it passes through a vein to your left atrium. Then it flows into the left ventricle, where it is pumped out, still full of oxygen, to the rest of your body. It is carried by several different blood vessels. Having dropped its oxygen, the blood returns to the right atrium, where it passes to the right ventricle. From here, the cycle starts again. The blood in your arteries going to the cells of your body contains oxygen. The blood in your veins returning to your heart contains carbon dioxide waste, which is taken back to the lungs and is breathed out.

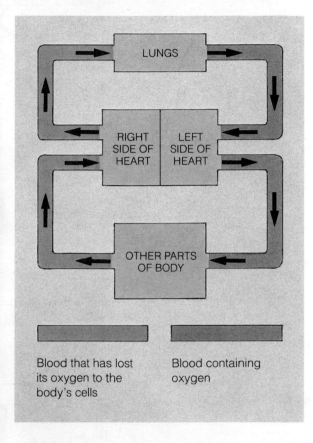

A simple diagram showing the pathway of blood through the body. This pathway is called the circulatory system.

TEST YOURSELF

1. What are the three kinds of blood vessels?
2. What is the function of capillaries?
3. What is the function of valves in your circulatory system?
4. Describe the pathway of blood through your body.

LUNGS AND BREATHING

Nutrients from food are broken down, or burned, releasing energy to the cells. This breakdown of nutrients, called cellular respiration, takes in oxygen and gives off carbon dioxide and water. You get oxygen from air you breathe in, and you breathe out carbon dioxide and water vapor.

When you breathe in, air goes into your mouth or nose and down a tube called the pharynx. Then it passes through your larynx (voice box) and into your windpipe, or trachea. This divides into two tubes called bronchi, which go into your lungs. Inside your lungs, the bronchi divide into smaller and smaller branches called bronchioles. These end in tiny air sacs (bags) called alveoli. The alveoli greatly increase the surface area of the lungs and are surrounded by capillaries.

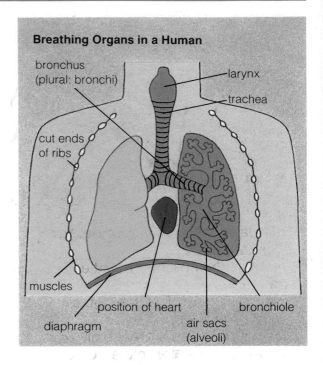

Breathing Organs in a Human

bronchus (plural: bronchi)

larynx

trachea

cut ends of ribs

muscles

position of heart

diaphragm

air sacs (alveoli)

bronchiole

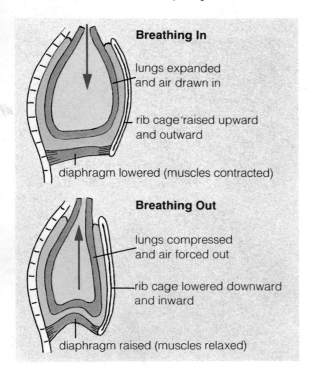

Breathing In

lungs expanded and air drawn in

rib cage raised upward and outward

diaphragm lowered (muscles contracted)

Breathing Out

lungs compressed and air forced out

rib cage lowered downward and inward

diaphragm raised (muscles relaxed)

Your lung surfaces are wet—oxygen must be dissolved before it can pass to cells of the body. When the alveoli fill with air, capillaries pick up oxygen and carry it away in the circulatory system to all parts of the body.

Below your lungs, there is a large sheet of muscle called the diaphragm. When you breathe in, your diaphragm contracts and flattens, and your ribs move up and out. This makes your chest cavity (space) larger, forcing your lungs to inflate (get larger) to fill the space. This makes air rush in. When you breathe out, the muscles between your ribs tighten. Your rib cage moves down and in. Your diaphragm relaxes and becomes dome-shaped. These two processes make your chest cavity smaller, forcing your lungs to collapse. This pushes the air out of your lungs, mouth, and nose.

ACTIVITY

LUNG CAPACITY

YOU NEED

- **a large bowl**
- **a 1-gallon milk bottle or other see-through container with cap**
- **plastic tubing**
- **antiseptic wipes**
- **a marking pen**

1 Put water in the bowl to a depth of about 2 inches.
2 Completely fill the milk bottle with water.
3 Put on the cap. Turn the bottle upside down in the bowl.
4 Remove the cap underwater. This will keep the water in the bottle.
5 Insert the tubing under the rim of the bottle. Make sure that the top of the bottle stays underwater. Wipe the other end of the tubing with an antiseptic wipe.

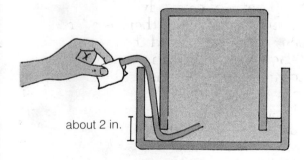

about 2 in.

6 Take a big breath and hold it.
7 Put the end of the tubing in your mouth. Breathe out, through the tube, until you have completely emptied your lungs.

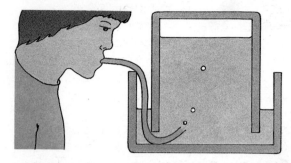

8 Pinch the tube as soon as you have finished to prevent the water from rushing out.
9 Ask a friend to mark the water level on the side of the container. Write your initials beside the mark.

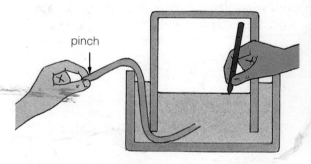

pinch

10 Compare your lung capacity with that of your friends. Who has the largest lung capacity? Does the smallest person have the smallest lung capacity?

TEST YOURSELF

1. What is cellular respiration? What are the waste products?
2. What happens in your chest when you breathe in?
3. What happens in your chest when you breathe out?

YOUR BRAIN

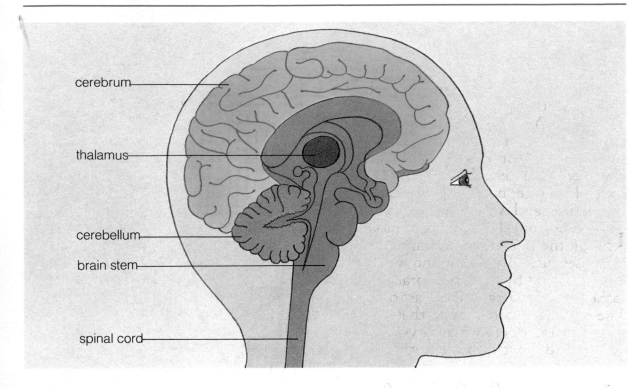

Your brain controls your nervous system, which means that it also controls your whole body. For this reason, some people think of the brain as being like a complicated central computer. Most of the brain's control is involuntary (see page 34). For example, heartbeat, body temperature, breathing, muscle tension, and other body systems are all controlled by the brain. Your brain also controls your voluntary actions, such as running, walking, writing, or reading. Besides these bodily actions, your brain helps you to learn, think, dream, imagine, remember, and make judgments.

There are three parts to your brain: the cerebrum, cerebellum, and brain stem. The cerebrum is the largest part and is found at the top of the brain. It is divided into halves called the

A diagram showing the main areas of the human brain: the cerebrum, the cerebellum, and the brain stem.

cerebral hemispheres. Each half controls the senses and movement in the opposite half of the body. For example, your left cerebral hemisphere controls the right side of your body. Both hemispheres control your breathing and swallowing. Your left hemisphere controls reading, writing, speech, and any special skills that you have. However, if you are left-handed, your right hemisphere controls reading, writing, and speech.

The front of your cerebrum helps control how you get along with other people. It helps you control your emotions and behave appropriately in company. The back of your cerebrum tells you about light, shade, shape, color and patterns. The lower part is for hearing, smell, and anger, fear, and sexual behavior.

Your cerebellum is below the cerebrum and controls your posture, which is the correct positioning of the parts of your body, and coordinates movement. Your brain stem joins your cerebrum and cerebellum to your spinal cord. It controls the nerves of your head and neck. It also helps to control balance, breathing, blood circulation, and wakefulness. All your nerve cells from the spinal cord pass through the brain stem. Complicated processes such as thought and memory are controlled by the whole brain, rather than by a particular part of it. The brain is so complicated that scientists and doctors may never understand exactly how it works.

This girl's brain plays a vital role in helping her to balance.

ACTIVITY

1 Choose a simple task, such as opening a door.
2 Perform that task. As you do it, think about every stage—the information you are receiving and the decisions you are making. What does your brain tell your body to do?
3 Write down everything that you thought of. Make an instruction sheet, describing each stage of your task.
4 See if a friend can perform the task properly by following your instructions.

TEST YOURSELF

1. What are the three parts of your brain?
2. What does the left cerebral hemisphere control if you are right-handed?
3. What does the back of your brain control?
4. What does your brain stem do?

YOUR NERVOUS SYSTEM

Your nervous system is one of the most complicated parts of your body. Without it, you would not be able to survive, because it helps the parts of your body to communicate with each other. It consists of the brain, spinal cord, and sensory and motor systems.

The sensory system is the part that picks up information, such as light from the eye. It is a vast network of nerve cells called neurons, which pick up stimuli (information) through nerve endings. Each stimulus is turned into an electrical impulse, which travels along the neuron. Usually, the impulse is passed on to another neuron in the network. The neurons have fine branches at one end called dendrites, and these transmit (pass on) the information to the next neuron. Eventually, the impulse goes to your spinal cord, which is found inside your spine. This cord is connected to your brain, so that all information is taken there to be interpreted.

Once your brain has found out what the electrical message means, it must tell your body how to react. This is when the motor system starts its work. Electrical impulses telling your body what to do are sent from the brain down the spinal cord. They pass into another huge network of motor neurons, which work in exactly the same way as the sensory neurons. The only difference is that the motor neurons usually end up in a completely different part of your body.

There are two types of action that your brain and nervous system cause. One is called voluntary and means actions that you control, although you may not be aware of it. Some examples are walking, running, and writing. Most of your actions are involuntary, or automatic. This means that you cannot control them in any way. One example of this is your reflexes. You may have had these tested by a doctor to see if your nervous system is working properly. Cross one leg over the other in a sitting position, and get a friend to tap you gently with the side of the hand just below your knee. Your

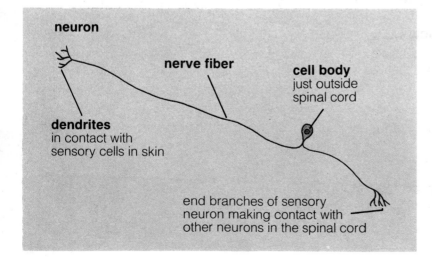

neuron

nerve fiber

cell body
just outside
spinal cord

dendrites
in contact with
sensory cells in skin

end branches of sensory
neuron making contact with
other neurons in the spinal cord

A diagram showing a sensory neuron. It takes messages from sensory cells to the spinal cord.

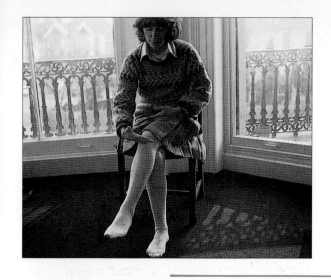

The woman is testing her "knee-jerk" reflex. It shows whether that part of her nervous system is working properly.

leg should jerk slightly. A different type of reflex action occurs when saliva flows into your mouth if you are hungry and smell food.

In general, nerve cells cannot be repaired or replaced. For this reason, injury to the nervous system is very serious. A person can be paralyzed by injury to the spinal cord. Injury to the brain can be fatal.

ACTIVITY

INVOLUNTARY ACTIONS

YOU NEED

- **a well-lighted room**
- **a watch with a second hand**
- **a knife**
- **a cutting board**
- **an onion**

1 Work with a friend. If you wear glasses, take them off.
2 Ask your friend to count how many times you blink in one minute. For this experiment to work, you must try not to control your eyelid movement. Try not to think about it.

3 Cut an onion into small pieces on the cutting board. Get your friend to count how many times you blink in one minute. Has your blinking increased?

	number of blinks in 1 minute
without onion	
with onion	

Onion juice comes through the air as a vapor. It irritates your eyes, making them sting. Your brain tells your eyelids to blink faster, bathing your eyes with tears that wash them. It also tells glands in the corners of your eyes to produce more tears, with the same result. Many involuntary actions, like this one, are for safety.

TEST YOURSELF

1. What are the different parts of your nervous system?
2. What is a stimulus? Name two.
3. Describe an involuntary action.

YOUR SKIN

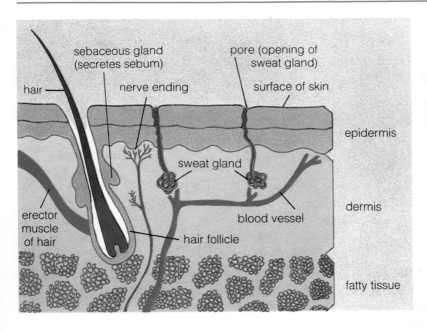

A diagram showing a cross section of the skin.

Labels on the diagram:
- hair
- sebaceous gland (secretes sebum)
- nerve ending
- pore (opening of sweat gland)
- surface of skin
- epidermis
- sweat gland
- dermis
- blood vessel
- erector muscle of hair
- hair follicle
- fatty tissue

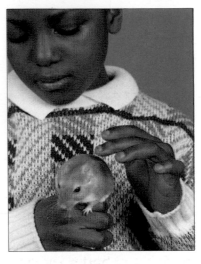

The nerves in the boy's fingertips sense the softness of the hamster's fur.

Your body is covered by an organ called skin. Skin protects your body from harmful substances, bacteria, and viruses, as well as it protects against ultraviolet rays from the sun. It is waterproof, keeping your body fluids in and water out. It has two layers—the epidermis and the dermis. The epidermis is a thin outer layer of cells, some of which are dead. The inner layer, or dermis, contains muscles, nerves, capillaries, and glands.

Because you make so many different movements, you skin is elastic, or stretchy, preventing it from splitting. It is especially elastic over your joints, such as the elbow. Glands secrete an oily substance called sebum, which helps keep the skin elastic.

Your skin helps to keep your body temperature constant. Most people's temperature is 98.6°F. When you are ill, your body temperature may go up or down. When you are overheated, your skin automatically cools you. Sweat glands secrete sweat. When it evaporates, it takes away extra heat from your body, and you cool down.

When the outside temperature is cold, tiny capillaries constrict (close up), making your skin look blue. This cuts down the blood supply to your skin and keeps heat from being lost. You also get "goose bumps," which are caused when tiny hairs on your skin are raised by little muscles. The goose bumps are little bunches of muscle. The erect hairs trap a layer of warm air next to your skin.

Your skin also contains nerves that tell you about your surroundings through the sense of touch. You can feel heat and cold, as well as textures such as rough and smooth. Some parts of the skin have more never endings than others. For example, the skin covering your fingertips has many nerve endings, so your fingertips are more sensitive than your knees.

ACTIVITY

THE SENSITIVITY OF YOUR SKIN

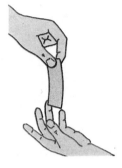

YOU NEED

- **a wide range of small objects with different textures**
- **a blindfold**

1 Work with a friend.
2 Make a chart showing the name of each different object and the areas of your skin that you are going to test. Some examples are your fingertips, back of forearm, forehead, lips, knees, and toes.

Area	Object 1	Object 2	Object 3
fingertips			
forehead			
lips			

3 Ask a friend to blindfold you.
4 Feel each object in turn with your fingertips. Your friend should mark a check for each correct answer and a cross for each wrong answer.

5 Ask your friend to rub each object in turn against the back of your forearm. Do this in a different order from the one that was followed in step 4.

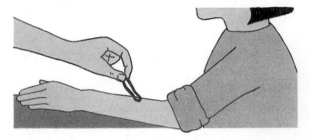

6 Repeat this for the other areas that you have chosen to test. Remember to ask your friend to give you the objects in a different order each time.
7 Look at your results. Which part that you tested has the most sensitive skin? Which has the least sensitive? Can you think of reasons why?

TEST YOURSELF

1. How is it helpful that your skin is elastic? What helps to keep it elastic?
2. Explain how your skin protects your body.
3. What happens to your skin when you are cold?
4. What happens to your skin when you are hot?

YOUR SENSES

Every moment of your life, your body finds out about its surroundings and makes decisions that avoid injury and death. To help you do this, you have five senses. You have already found out about your sense of touch (see page 37). The other senses are hearing, sight, taste, and smell.

Your sense organs are all different, but they work in a similar way. They have sensitive cells that pick up information from the outside world. They pass this information to the brain through nerves. Your brain then interprets the messages and tells your body what to do. For example, it might tell you to move your hand away from a hot surface. This all happens very quickly—in a few millionths of a second.

Your eyes are your organs of sight. Light is the stimulus that causes you to see. It passes through a transparent tissue called the cornea, at the front of your eye. Inside, it passes through a clear jelly to the lens, then through more clear jelly to the retina. This is where the light-sensitive cells are

found. They send messages to your brain along the optic nerve. Your brain interprets these messages, telling you what you can see.

Your hearing organs are the ears. The stimulus is sound, which is pressure waves in the air. They cause the eardrum to vibrate, and this is passed on by a system of three tiny bones to your inner ear. Here, hairlike sensitive cells pick up the vibrations and turn them into electrical messages to be sent to your brain.

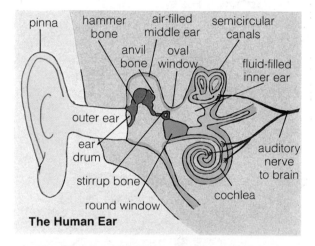

The Human Ear

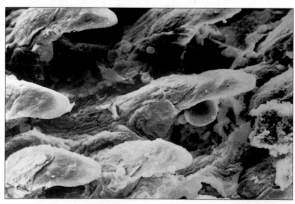

The taste buds on the tongue shown through a microscope.

The Human Eye

Your senses of taste and smell work in a similar way. Chemicals are the stimuli, and they dissolve in water, either in your nose or on your tongue. Hollows in your nose have sensitive cells that detect the chemicals and send messages to your brain. On your tongue, you have taste buds, which are sensitive cells. Different areas detect salt, sour, sweet, and bitter chemicals. They send messages to the brain. Your tongue and nose work together to help you to find out what you are eating or drinking.

ACTIVITY

SMELL AND TASTE

YOU NEED

- **a kitchen knife**
- **a cutting board**
- **an onion**
- **an apple**
- **a pear**
- **a blindfold**
- **running water**
- **a cup**

1 Work with a friend.
2 Very carefully cut up the onion, apple, and pear into small pieces. Keep them separate.

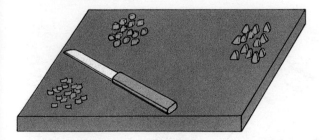

3 Ask your friend to blindfold you.
4 Get your friend to choose two different pieces of chopped food. Your friend must put one piece in your mouth while holding the other piece under your nose. Smell and chew at the same time. What do you think you are eating?

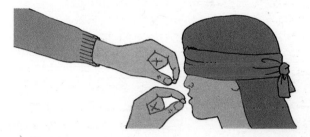

5 Rinse your mouth well with water. Do the same thing with two more pieces of chopped food.
6 Try all combinations of smelling and tasting the chopped food.
7 Did you always guess correctly? Is one sense better than the other?
8 Repeat the activity with your friend blindfolded. Were your results the same as your friend's?

TEST YOURSELF

1. How many different senses do you have?
2. How are sense organs similar to each other?
3. Describe how one of your sense organs works.

HORMONES

You have already found out that your brain and nervous system control your body. However, many of your body's activities are also controlled by chemical messengers called hormones. These are carried through the body in tiny quantities by the blood. Most hormones are made by special organs called endocrine glands. Some hormones affect every cell in your body. Others have only one special task.

There are five main endocrine glands: pituitary, pancreas, adrenal, thyroid and parathyroid, and sex glands (testes and ovaries—see page 42). The pituitary gland makes many hormones. One hormone controls growth. Your body will produce less of it when you are fully grown. The front of the pituitary gland is called the anterior lobe, and it controls your thyroid, adrenal, and sex glands. The back (posterior lobe) controls the ways in which your blood vessels and parts of your kidneys work, and the breasts and uterus (see page 42) in women. Your pancreas controls the amount of sugar going to your cells.

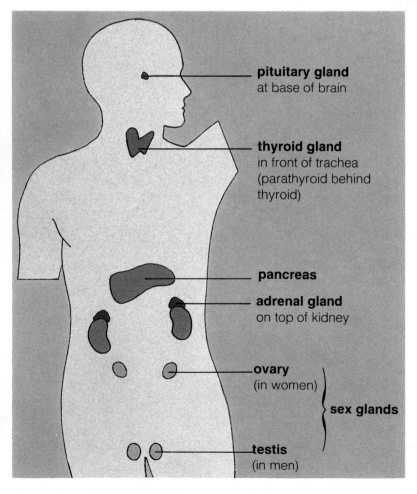

A diagram showing the main endocrine glands in the human body.

pituitary gland
at base of brain

thyroid gland
in front of trachea
(parathyroid behind
thyroid)

pancreas

adrenal gland
on top of kidney

ovary
(in women)

sex glands

testis
(in men)

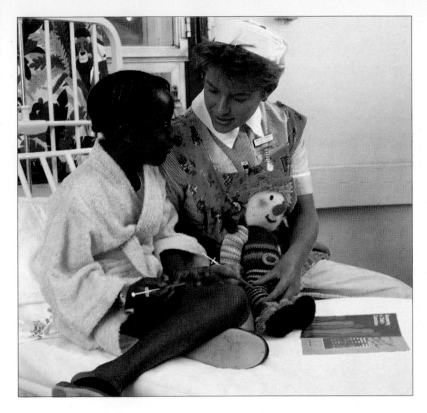

This girl is diabetic. The nurse is teaching her to inject herself with insulin. She will probably have to do this once a day for the rest of her life.

You may have heard of an illness called diabetes. A diabetic person's pancreas cannot produce a hormone called insulin. He or she may need a special diet and injections of insulin so that the correct amount of sugar goes to each cell. If the amount of sugar is too high or too low, the diabetic quickly becomes ill and may even die.

Your adrenal glands have two parts: the cortex and the medulla. The cortex controls levels of salt in your body and helps to make your cells resistant to injury. It also helps to control the amount of protein (see page 16) that is built up in your body. The medulla makes a hormone called adrenaline, which prepares you for quick action if you are frightened.

Your thyroid gland controls the rate at which body cells break down food and get energy. There are four small parathyroid glands (attached to the thyroid). They are the only glands not controlled by the pituitary. They seem to have only one task: controlling the amounts of calcium and phosphorus in your body.

TEST YOURSELF

1. What are hormones?
2. Which endocrine gland produces adrenaline? What does it do?
3. Which are the only glands that are not controlled by the pituitary?
4. What causes a person to be diabetic?

REPRODUCTION

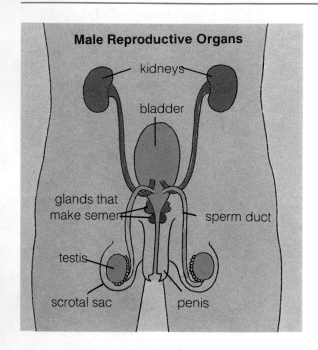

Male Reproductive Organs

kidneys

bladder

glands that make semen

sperm duct

testis

scrotal sac

penis

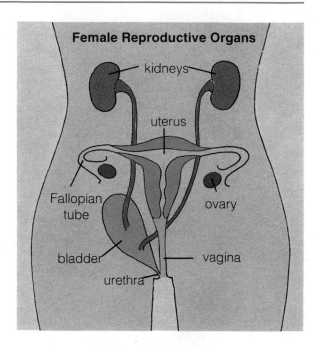

Female Reproductive Organs

kidneys

uterus

Fallopian tube

ovary

bladder

vagina

urethra

Humans do not live forever, but they replace themselves. They do this by reproducing. When cells reproduce themselves (see page 8), they make an exact copy. If you look at your family, you will see that we do not make exact copies of ourselves. This is because children get a mixture of characteristics from both parents.

Men and women have sex cells which join to form the first cells of a baby. Information in the sex cells determines many traits of the child. It determines the child's eye, hair, and skin coloring. It even dictates how tall the child will grow. Other information determines personality and talents.

A baby girl is born with sex cells, which are stored in the ovaries. When she is about eleven years old (although this varies), she reaches puberty. This means that she begins to be able to reproduce. Every month, one sex cell,

an ovum (egg) is released from an ovary and travels down the Fallopian tube to the womb, or uterus. During that month, a lining of blood builds up in the uterus. Usually, the egg and blood passes out of the girl's body about fourteen days later. This is called menstruation.

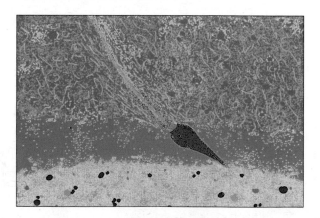

A sperm that has just passed through the outer layer of an egg during fertilization.

A baby boy is born with two testes. When he reaches puberty, they start to produce sex cells called sperm. These look like tiny tadpoles.

For a man and a woman to have a baby, one ovum must join with one sperm. This happens during sexual intercourse. Here, the man's penis fills with blood, so that it can enter the woman's vagina. Millions of sperm are carried in a fluid called semen out the end of his penis, and the sperm swim into the uterus and up the Fallopian tubes. In one of these tubes, the sperm meet the ovum, and one of them joins with it. This is called fertilization. The rest of the sperm die. The egg moves down the Fallopian tube and into the uterus. There, it sticks to the blood lining and develops into a baby.

The baby is attached to the lining of the womb by a special cord protruding from its abdomen. Your belly button is the scar left by this cord. Food and oxygen pass through this tube to the baby, and waste products pass back to the mother. The baby floats in a liquid inside the uterus. This liquid protects it from injury.

After about forty weeks (nine months), the baby sends chemical messages that tell the mother's body that it is ready to be born. The uterus, which is very muscular, starts to contract (tighten), pushing the baby out through the mother's vagina. This is called labor. When the baby is born, it starts to breathe and its cord is cut.

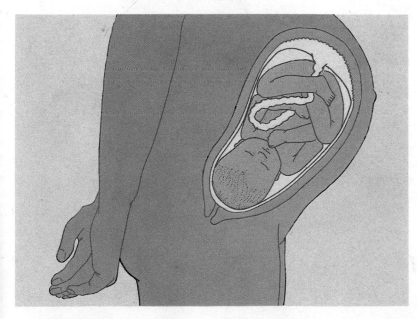

A diagram showing a baby inside its mother's uterus, shortly before it is born.

TEST YOURSELF

1. Where are a woman's sex cells found? Where are those of a man found?
2. Why are children not exact copies of their parents?
3. What is menstruation?
4. How does a baby inside its mother get its food and oxygen?

LEADING A HEALTHY LIFE

There are many things that you can do to make sure that you stay as healthy as possible. You have already learned which foods you need to eat (see page 16). Your muscles and heart need to stay in good condition, so you should exercise. Walking quickly for about twenty minutes, three times a week, is thought to keep you in good shape. Climbing the stairs instead of using the elevator is a good idea. Swimming is also good exercise for the whole body.

It is very important to get plenty of sleep. Most adults need about six to eight hours of sleep every day, and children need more. People who continually get less sleep than they need become tired, irritable, and cannot think properly. This makes it harder for them to do their work and enjoy life. You should also avoid alcohol, smoking, and drugs.

Sometimes your body does not work properly. For example, some people get cancer, a disease in which cells make too many copies of themselves. Some diseases are caused by bacteria and viruses. Bacteria, tiny living things, cause pneumonia and tetanus. Viruses are much smaller than bacteria and can cause colds as well as serious diseases, such as AIDS. You probably had injections to prevent many different diseases. Other problems can be cured by your doctor. If you feel ill, tell your parents.

Some people go to the doctor for regular checkups, to make sure that they are in good health. The doctor will weigh you, check your blood pressure and pulse, listen to your heart and lungs, and sometimes do other tests, such as blood tests. The doctor can pick up signs of ill health and tell you what to do about it.

It is very important to your health to get enough sleep.

You should also visit your dentist regularly to prevent or treat tooth and gum disease.

Finally, remember to keep your body clean. Keep your home clean and get plenty of fresh air. Prepare, eat, and store your food in clean places. Make sure that the food you buy is fresh, and always look for the "sell by" date on packaged food. Remember: you have only one body, and you will have a better life if you keep it healthy.

This little girl is sick. Her father is giving her some medicine prescribed by the doctor. It is important to go to the doctor if you are ill.

ACTIVITY

A HEALTH SURVEY

YOU NEED

- **several friends**

1 Make up a survey about health. For example, you could ask people how much sleep they get, how often they are sick, how often they go to the dentist, how often they brush their teeth, and what exercise they get.
2 Give your survey to several friends.
3 Use what you have learned to see if your friends lead a healthy life.

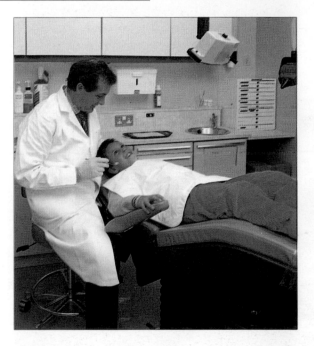

It is important to visit the dentist regularly.

TEST YOURSELF

1. How can you help to keep your heart and muscles in good condition?
2. What sort of tests will your doctor do at a general checkup?
3. What happens to people who do not get enough sleep?

Glossary

Abdomen The part of the body (trunk) between the diaphragm and the pelvis.

Acid A solution that is below pH7.

Alkali A solution that is above pH7.

Bladder An organ that is like a bag. It usually means the organ that stores urine in the body.

Bowel The lower part of the digestive system.

Breast-feeding Giving milk to a baby from the breasts rather than from a bottle.

Calcium An essential element in bones and teeth.

Cancer A dangerous growth of cells in the body, which in some cases can cause death.

Cavity A spot of decay in a tooth.

Constipation This is caused when the bowels are not working properly, and waste material is stored in the body too long.

Dental floss A special thread used to remove pieces of food from between the teeth.

Diaphragm A large muscle that separates the chest from the abdomen.

Digestion The breakdown of food into simpler chemicals.

Fiber Food that cannot be digested but is a very important part of our diet.

Fibrin Fine threads formed in the blood when it is exposed to air. It is responsible for blood clotting.

Immunization A treatment to prevent disease, usually given by injection.

Kidneys Two small organs at the back of the body that are used to filter and clean the blood. They make urine.

Ligaments Tough, fibrous tissue that holds bones together.

Lens (of the eye) A clear material that focuses light rays onto the retina.

Optic nerve The bundle of nerves that sends electrical messages from the eye to the brain.

Organ A part of the body that carries out a particular task.

Oxygen A gas that makes up about 20 percent of the air. It is essential for respiration in animals and humans.

Protein A complex substance containing nitrogen, carbon, hydrogen, oxygen, and usually sulfur and phosphorus that is essential for growth and repair in the body.

Pulse A beat that can be felt under the skin. It corresponds to the heartbeat.

Reflex An involuntary, or automatic, nervous reaction.

Tendon A fibrous material holding muscles to bone.

Tissue A collection of cells that are similar. Several different types of tissues may make up an organ.

Trunk The body of an animal or a human, not including the head or limbs.

Urine A liquid that contains waste products. It is made by the kidneys.

Whole-grain products Foods that are made from the complete grain. No parts have been removed. They are usually high in dietary fiber.

Books to Read

Asimov, Isaac. *How Did We Find out About the Brain?* Walker, 1987.

Bailey, Donna. *Health Facts Series,* 8 vols., Steck-Vaughn, 1991.

Collinson, Alan. *Choosing Health.* Steck-Vaughn, 1991.

Conway, Lorraine. *Body Systems.* Good Apple, 1984.

Crump, Donald J., ed. *Your Wonderful Body.* National Geographic, 1982.

Fichter, George. *Cells.* Watts, 1986.

Gamlin, Linda. *The Human Body.* Watts, 1988.

Ward, Brian. *The Lungs and Breathing.* Watts, 1982.

Wong, Ovid. *Your Body and How It Works.* Childrens, 1986.

Picture Acknowledgments

The author and publishers would like to thank the following for allowing illustrations to be reproduced in this book: Ron Boardman 8, 12, 14, 24, 28, 38; St. Mary's Hospital Medical School 11; Science Photo Library 26, 41, 42; Topham *cover* (left); Wayland Picture Library *frontispiece,* 17 (Trevor Hill), 18 (Peter Stiles), 34, 36, 45 (top/Paul Seheult) 45 (bottom/Trevor Hill); ZEFA *cover* (top right), 44. All artwork is by Jenny Hughes.

Index

First published in 1991 by
Wayland (Publishers) Ltd.

© Copyright 1991 Wayland
(Publishers) Ltd